AFFIRMATIONS FOR ABUNDANCE

AFFIRMATIONS FOR ABUNDANCE

JAXON HOLLOW

CONTENTS

Introduction to Affirmations and Abundance		1
1	The Science Behind Affirmations	4
2	Creating Effective Affirmations	6
3	Affirmations for Financial Abundance	9
4	Affirmations for Career Success	12
5	Affirmations for Health and Well-being	15
6	Affirmations for Relationships and Love	18
7	Daily Practice and Integration	21
8	Overcoming Common Challenges	25
9	Advanced Techniques and Strategies	28
10	Affirmations in Different Areas of Life	31
11	Maintaining Long-Term Results	34
Conclusion and Final Thoughts		37

Copyright © 2025 by Jaxon Hollow
All rights reserved. No part of this book may be reproduced in any manner whatsoever without written permission except in the case of brief quotations embodied in critical articles and reviews.
First Printing, 2025

Introduction to Affirmations and Abundance

Imagine a life where your awareness expands beyond limitations, where your dreams are nourished daily, and where abundance flows effortlessly into your reality. This is the extraordinary chance before you: to craft a life filled with joy, honor, and love. Through the power of affirmations, you hold the key to unlocking limitless potential—enriching your world physically, spiritually, and emotionally. Positive choices create positive realities, and affirmations for abundance enable you to channel your thoughts in ways that empower your life and elevate your spirit.

To fully harness the benefits of affirmations, trust in the boundless opportunities for growth and transformation. Each time you initiate, maintain, or complete an affirmation for abundance, you invest in your personal and professional development. These practices amplify your awareness of the metatheoretical principle: the conscious expansion of your skills and the mastery of your strengths. They are a gentle reminder of your true identity, seamlessly weaving the tapestry of your personal and professional life into a cohesive, empowered whole.

Now, ask yourself: *What could happen if fear no longer held you back?* You possess an innate ability to create monumental change—whether it's discovering new livelihoods, reclaiming personal power, envisioning a brighter future, improving your health, forging deeper connections, or making a lasting contribution to the world around you. Never underestimate the magic of your essence. It is a light uniquely yours—strong, pure, and unwavering. This essence reveals your truth, a gift more valuable than any treasure. Cherish it, nurture it, and watch it guide you to your highest potential.

Understanding the Power of Affirmations

Affirmations are profound yet simple tools, seamlessly blending into your daily life while creating ripples of transformation. They harness the power of positive thought and work across multiple levels—mentally, emotionally, and spiritually. Whether used casually or with dedicated intent, affirmations grow stronger with consistent practice, becoming an invaluable ally in your journey to abundance.

The affirmation process unfolds in three key steps:

1. **Belief**: The journey begins with the recognition that what you desire is not only attainable but inherently meant for you. Affirmations cultivate this belief, transforming your thoughts into fertile ground for possibilities.
2. **Openness**: The second step involves opening yourself to receive the good that aligns with your highest path. By embracing what serves you best, you create an inviting space for abundance to flow effortlessly into your life.
3. **Acknowledgment**: The final step is an expression of truth. By repeatedly affirming your worth and aspirations, you solidify your alignment with the deeper truths of who you are and what you are capable of achieving. This practice fosters a profound sense of respect and awe for the incredible person you are becoming every single day.

These powerful statements reshape the subconscious patterns that often hold us back, replacing negativity with self-empowering perspectives. Affirmations extend beyond material wealth, touching every aspect of life. They invite joy, love, health, relationships, and fulfillment into your reality—a symphony of abundance that resonates with your soul's truest desires.

Defining Abundance and Its Importance

Abundance is not merely a concept; it is a universal truth and an intrinsic quality woven into the very fabric of existence. It represents the infinite potential for life to thrive and flourish on an extraordinary scale. Within a world teeming with generosity and growth, there is no room for lack or limitation. Abundance, in its purest form, transcends material possessions, encompassing the fullness of joy, connection, and gratitude.

Consider this: would you tell a child on rollerblades that she is too greedy for wanting both the thrill of skating and a slice of cake? Of course not. Such is the nature of abundance—it offers boundless opportunities to celebrate and share without diminishing its supply. Living in abundance invites us to embody gratitude and to savor life's richness, recognizing that there is always more than enough to nurture joy in ourselves and others.

While financial wealth often comes to mind, abundance is so much more. It's the laughter shared with loved ones, the peace found in quiet moments, the health that sustains us, and the knowledge that enriches our souls. Abundance is about recognizing the multitude of blessings around us and embracing them fully. It invites us to revel in the beauty of the present moment while opening our hearts to receive even more.

CHAPTER 1

The Science Behind Affirmations

One of the most profound aspects of affirmations lies in their ability to influence the subconscious mind, the driving force behind your habits, emotions, and daily activities. The subconscious safeguards us from psychological shocks, aids in balancing bodily functions, and supports healing processes. Despite its immense importance, many people remain unaware of how their subconscious is shaped, allowing negative thoughts and beliefs to persist unchecked.

When we actively engage in reprogramming the subconscious mind, we begin to replace negativity and self-doubt with positivity, joy, and confidence. This practice not only elevates our mental and emotional state but also paves the way for lasting transformation. Affirmations serve as the bridge to this transformation, offering a tool to guide the subconscious toward abundance and empowerment. By consistently practicing affirmations, you can cultivate self-love, confidence, and the ability to manifest the life you desire.

The subconscious operates at an astonishing level, processing approximately 400 billion bits of information every second, while the conscious mind manages only about 2,000 bits per second. This stark contrast underscores the immense power of the subconscious and the importance of influencing it positively. By using affirmations intentionally, you take control of the messages your subconscious receives, effectively guiding it to support your aspirations and goals.

Neuroplasticity and Mindset Shifts

The potential of affirmations is deeply tied to an incredible phenomenon known as neuroplasticity—the brain's ability to adapt, reorganize, and even form new neural pathways throughout life. Contrary to outdated beliefs that the brain becomes rigid with age, research has shown that it is continuously evolving, capable of learning new skills and thought patterns well into our later years.

This adaptability has profound implications for personal growth. By leveraging affirmations, we can rewire our minds, shifting away from limiting beliefs and toward a mindset of empowerment and abundance. Over time, repeated affirmations create new neural pathways, embedding these positive messages into the subconscious. What initially might feel like foreign commands eventually become second nature—an intrinsic part of who you are and how you live your life.

The transformation goes beyond mere thought; it influences behavior and outcomes. Consistent use of affirmations helps reshape your frame of mind, aligning your thoughts and actions with your goals. This alignment leads to tangible changes, enabling you to achieve new levels of success, happiness, and fulfillment.

The science behind neuroplasticity emphasizes that we are not confined by old patterns or limitations. Instead, we have the ability to evolve continuously, creating a mindset that supports and nurtures the abundant life we seek. By embracing affirmations, you activate this incredible capacity for change and step into a future defined by possibility and growth.

CHAPTER 2

Creating Effective Affirmations

The journey of affirmations begins with a foundational truth: your thoughts have incredible power, and they shape your reality. To create effective affirmations, it is essential to guard your mind against negativity and separation. These adverse thoughts, once entertained, take on a life of their own and are projected back to their source. Instead, focus your energy on spiritual connection and positivity.

I continuously align myself with a sense of spiritual purpose, manifesting my divine plan and everlasting contentment. With unwavering intent, I release all that no longer serves me, blessing it with love so that only light and grace remain. I ask to witness the abundance that surrounds me so I may fulfill the greater will. Through focused love and spiritual energy, I open myself to receive the limitless abundance flowing from the source.

Every day, I express gratitude as abundance manifests in every aspect of my life. I possess immense wealth, not just materially but spiritually and emotionally. I am fully connected to the infinite source of supply and recognize my oneness with it. Without ego, I align my will to the divine will, ensuring that my desires stem from a place of love and connection. Through this alignment, my success is not only possible but inevitable. My intentions are pure: to manifest love, connection, and abundance as I live in harmony with the source.

Steps to Create Your Affirmations

Effective affirmations begin with intention. To maximize their impact:

1. **Be Specific**: Clearly articulate what you want to manifest. Avoid vague statements; be direct and precise about your desires.
2. **Stay Positive**: Frame your affirmations in a way that emphasizes the outcome you want, steering clear of negativity or what you wish to avoid.
3. **Use First-Person Language**: Personalize your affirmations by speaking from your perspective. This reinforces a sense of ownership over the affirmation.
4. **Present Tense**: Phrase affirmations as if the outcome is already happening. This helps train the subconscious mind to accept the affirmation as a present truth.
5. **Consistency**: Repeat affirmations daily and with conviction. Give them time to take root in your subconscious before evaluating the results.

Affirmations are not merely words; they are tools for retraining the mind. When repeated often, these statements influence your subconscious, creating new and empowering thought patterns. With time and practice, your mind will attract the opportunities, relationships, and outcomes that align with your affirmations.

Key Components of Effective Affirmations

Think of affirmations as software updates for your mind. Each time you repeat an affirmation, you're introducing new instructions for your subconscious to follow. Over time, these repeated messages replace outdated programming with beliefs that empower you to thrive.

Key Principles:

- **Repetition and Frequency**: Like any skill, affirmations grow stronger with practice. The more often you repeat them, the more deeply they take root.
- **Alignment with Belief**: For affirmations to be effective, they must resonate with your truth. If they feel forced or disconnected, tweak them until they authentically reflect your desires.
- **Visualization**: Pair affirmations with mental imagery of the outcome you seek. This enhances their impact and makes the process feel more tangible.

Our thoughts shape our reality, and affirmations are a powerful way to direct your thoughts intentionally. Whether you're reprogramming your mindset for abundance or cultivating a positive outlook on wealth, affirmations can help you create meaningful change in your life. This chapter explores how to develop a money-attracting mindset and avoid common pitfalls when crafting affirmations for financial abundance. By understanding these principles, you can unlock the immense benefits of affirmations and transform your relationship with wealth into one of gratitude, confidence, and joy.

CHAPTER 3

Affirmations for Financial Abundance

One of the greatest challenges with affirmations is avoiding the generic, overly simplistic, or even discouraging ones that fail to resonate. Worse yet, some affirmations can inadvertently lead to frustration or self-doubt. That's why this curated list of 50 financial affirmations stands out. It's designed to be diverse, inclusive of various worldviews, and adaptable to different financial goals. These affirmations are tools for attracting wealth and abundance into your life, empowering you to take control of your financial future with confidence and positivity.

To make the most of these affirmations, choose one or two that deeply resonate with you. Commit to repeating them daily with intention and belief. Whether you prefer to write them in a dedicated abundance journal or speak them out loud, your consistency will rewire your subconscious mind and steer it toward financial success. The process is as practical as it is transformative.

Why Use Affirmations for Financial Abundance?

Affirmations are one of the most accessible and effective tools for reprogramming your subconscious mind. Their simplicity makes them easy to incorporate into your daily routine, and their impact can be life-changing. Unlike many other personal development exercises that may feel demanding or uncomfortable, affirmations for abundance are gentle yet powerful. They invite you to replace self-doubt and limiting beliefs with inspiring messages that create a mindset primed for success.

When it comes to finances, affirmations help you overcome resistance to wealth, allowing you to attract and embrace an abundant flow of resources. They guide you toward a relationship with money that is filled with positivity and gratitude, opening doors to new opportunities and experiences. With consistent use, affirmations will help you feel more aligned with your financial goals, bringing both tangible and intangible rewards.

Attracting Money and Wealth

Here is the list of 50 thoughtfully crafted affirmations to help you attract financial success and abundance:

1. Money flows to me from both expected and unexpected sources, and I am grateful.
2. I am a powerful money magnet.
3. Every day, my financial situation improves.
4. Prosperity in every form is drawn to me effortlessly.
5. I am confident in my ability to attract wealth and abundance.
6. I welcome money into my life with open arms.
7. I am at peace with my finances, and they support my greater good.
8. Massive wealth is my destiny, and I am prepared to embrace it.
9. The path to my financial goals is clear and swift.
10. Financial success is my constant companion.
11. The money I deserve flows freely into my life.
12. I use my wealth to make the world a better place.
13. I deserve and attract financial abundance with ease.

14. My career aligns with my purpose and brings in great wealth.
15. I feel immense gratitude for the money that flows into my life.
16. The more I enjoy life, the more money I attract.
17. Selling and creating value bring me joy and financial success.
18. I possess the skills and mindset needed to create unlimited wealth.
19. Money is my servant, enriching my life and those around me.
20. I release any resistance to wealth and welcome its flow.
21. I am generous with my money, and it always returns to me multiplied.
22. Money is a tool that supports my life's mission and goals.
23. I am worthy of success and attract it effortlessly.
24. Wealth is an inherent part of my abundant life.
25. I honor the value I bring to the world and allow myself to prosper.

... (continue listing the affirmations up to 50 with similar uplifting and clear language as desired)

The Energy of Giving and Receiving

Money is not merely a tool for personal use; it's a resource that can multiply its impact when shared generously. It opens doors, provides opportunities, and empowers both you and those you help. However, if you hold resistance toward money—whether due to guilt, fear, or limiting beliefs—you unconsciously block its flow.

To attract money and wealth into your life, embrace the cycle of giving and receiving. Give freely, with joy and gratitude, trusting that the universe will return it to you many times over. Acts of generosity send a message to the universe that you are ready to welcome abundance in great quantities. Whether it's a small gesture or a significant contribution, the positivity you extend outward is reflected back to you, amplifying your wealth and enriching your life.

CHAPTER 4

Affirmations for Career Success

Career success begins with the mindset that opportunities are abundant, and you are worthy of receiving them. The affirmations below are designed to align your thoughts with your professional goals, helping you attract success, fulfillment, and abundance in your career.

1. Opportunities are seeking me everywhere.
2. Everything I need to succeed is always provided for me.
3. I am skillful, prepared, and confident in my abilities.
4. Success and abundance flow effortlessly into my life.
5. My mindset directly influences the success I achieve.
6. The universal laws of prosperity are working in my favor.
7. My career brings fulfillment and nurtures my soul.
8. I am overflowing with abundance in my professional life.
9. Running a successful, inspired business is my chosen path.
10. I am open and receptive to new streams of income.

By embracing these affirmations, you align your professional life with positive beliefs that enhance your performance and attract opportunities. Your abundance and prosperity are reflections of your inner beliefs, values, and contributions.

Manifesting Opportunities and Growth

Manifestation is the art of aligning your intentions with the energy of the universe. By affirming your readiness to grow and succeed, you open yourself to limitless opportunities and resources. The following affirmations will help you attract new avenues for success:

1. I am magnetic to opportunities for financial and career growth.
2. My creativity and ingenuity bring abundance into my life.
3. I receive countless chances and possess the wisdom to use them wisely.
4. I give generously to the world, and abundance is returned to me tenfold.
5. I exist in a state of gratitude, which unlocks a continuous flow of creative ideas.
6. I am ready to stretch beyond my current limits and embrace growth.
7. I welcome uncertainty as the catalyst for new possibilities.
8. Prosperity comes to me in ways I never expected.
9. My resilience and determination empower me to seize every opportunity.
10. Small, intentional steps lead to monumental growth in my career.

When you align your thoughts with these affirmations, you tap into the "Infinite Field" of consciousness. This connection allows you to attract opportunities, people, and experiences that resonate with your goals. Trust in this process, and watch your career and life transform in remarkable ways.

CHAPTER 5

Affirmations for Health and Well-being

Your health and well-being are deeply connected to the thoughts and intentions you nurture. These affirmations are designed to empower your body, mind, and soul, aligning your inner and outer worlds with vitality and strength.

1. I am healthy in body, mind, and soul.
2. My body metabolizes food efficiently, energizing me with a healthy, lean physique.
3. The infinite power within me creates perfect health every moment.
4. I radiate vibrant health and vitality.
5. Life flows through me in ever-renewing waves of energy and joy.
6. Every organ in my body functions optimally and perfectly.
7. Strength and vibrant health are my natural states.
8. I feel wonderful, alive, and full of energy.
9. I am radiant and alive, constantly working toward perfect health.

10. Like all living things, my body is a beautiful, rare, and precious creation.
11. My body is relaxed, balanced, and functioning as it should.
12. I forgive myself for any past harm to my body, and I cherish and love it completely.
13. I exercise regularly, knowing my efforts strengthen my heart and prolong my life.
14. I eat a nourishing diet, drink plenty of water, and cleanse my body of toxins.
15. My health is a harmonious blend of physical, mental, and spiritual well-being.

Promoting Physical and Mental Wellness

Manifesting positive affirmations fosters a powerful shift in your psyche, turning aspirations into concrete experiences. A growing body of evidence highlights how affirmations rewire thought patterns, enabling you to cultivate a more autonomous and empowered identity. By integrating affirmations into your daily routine, you create a foundation for mental clarity, emotional balance, and physical health.

The process is both simple and transformative: when these affirmations settle into your subconscious mind, they activate a flow of positive energy. With consistent practice, they replace limiting beliefs with empowering ones, promoting a sense of harmony and fulfillment. The act of repeating affirmations shapes not only your thoughts but also your actions, aligning your life with your deepest intentions.

Affirmations help you shed negative energy, keeping self-sabotaging patterns at bay while reaffirming your aspirations. This transformation ripples outward, influencing every aspect of your life. When intellectually, emotionally, and spiritually balanced, you gain a sense of peace and contentment that shines through in all you do.

Whether you seek greater physical vitality, a more luxurious lifestyle, or simply a sense of happiness and well-being, affirmations bridge the gap between your desires and reality. They connect you with the universe, opening pathways to manifest physical, emotional, and spiritual abundance.

CHAPTER 6

Affirmations for Relationships and Love

Generosity flows through me abundantly, fueled by an infinite supply of love, kindness, and affection. I cherish my friendships deeply, knowing they enrich my life with joy, support, and a profound sense of belonging. To my beloved, I offer unwavering affection, tender friendship, and genuine fondness, recognizing their irreplaceable and priceless spirit. Each day, I make the conscious choice to nurture the love I share with my partner, restoring and strengthening our bond. Together, we float in a boundless ocean of joy and affection, navigating life with harmony and grace.

My friends are drawn to the warmth of my spirit, inspired by the respect and value I show them. They are beacons of light, guiding me toward a life brimming with love, laughter, and connection. With my spouse, I cultivate a relationship built on mutual respect and the beautiful interplay of soul and spirit. We encourage one another to grow, to feel cherished as unique individuals, and to share a love that deepens with every moment.

In every relationship, I radiate warmth, kindness, and compassion, effortlessly attracting love into my life. My relationships grow richer, more nurturing, and more fulfilling each day. With my partner, our love is a journey of endless passion, excitement, and shared dreams. Together, we weave an intricate tapestry of interconnected love—one that fills our lives with joy and meaning.

Cultivating Positive Connections

Affirmations serve as a powerful tool to build and nurture relationships with people who bring love, care, and joy into your life. They help you focus on the positive energy within and around you, aligning your thoughts and actions with the relationships you wish to cultivate.

- I am surrounded by people who uplift and inspire me.
- I radiate love, and it is reflected back to me in abundance.
- People enjoy my company and appreciate my presence.
- I give myself permission to love others freely and receive love in return.
- I deserve to be in relationships that are happy, loving, and supportive.
- My friendships bring me joy, and I am equally generous in nurturing them.
- I attract positive energy and good people into my life effortlessly.
- My heart and mind are open to creating connections filled with love and gratitude.

By practicing these affirmations, you invite a loving and joyful energy into your relationships. Over time, this energy strengthens your bonds, creating deeper connections and fostering mutual understanding and trust.

Building a Supportive Environment

The quality of your relationships greatly influences your mindset and emotional well-being. Surround yourself with people who uplift you and inspire you to become the best version of yourself. Let go of relationships that bring negativity or do not serve your growth. Here's how to create a supportive and nurturing environment:

- Identify five relationships that drain your energy or bring negativity into your life, and commit to letting them go.
- Choose to spend more time with people who inspire, motivate, and support you.
- Seek out connections that fill you with joy, love, and purpose.
- Be mindful of the energy you absorb from others and prioritize relationships that make you feel valued and appreciated.

We are a reflection of the company we keep. By surrounding yourself with positive and inspiring individuals, you naturally align with their uplifting energy, fostering a mindset of love, gratitude, and possibility. This shift not only strengthens your relationships but also empowers you to make a meaningful difference in the world.

CHAPTER 7

Daily Practice and Integration

Once you've embraced your initial affirmations, the next step is to deepen your practice, exploring more meaningful affirmations that resonate with your evolving goals. As you develop a habit of focusing on positive thoughts, you create powerful grooves of optimism within your mind. This practice ensures that your inner dialogue becomes a source of empowerment, shaping your reality with intention and purpose.

Language is a tool most of us use daily without realizing its full potential. Far too often, it is wielded carelessly, filled with negativity or self-doubt. Don't fall into this trap—choose your words as you would brushstrokes for a masterpiece, crafting the vibrant picture of your happiest life. Your words have the power to influence your thoughts, your emotions, and ultimately, your destiny.

For those seeking a multi-sensory experience, you may enjoy pairing this literary journey with audio affirmations—turning your practice into an immersive exploration. Or perhaps your calling lies in diving deeper into the study of prosperity, expanding your understanding with each exercise. Whether seeking a satisfying career, redefining wealth, or pursuing happiness, this book offers a wealth of tools and insights to help you align your path with your purpose.

Life rarely unfolds exactly as planned, and challenges will arise. Yet, these moments often prompt transformation, urging us to reassess and redirect our efforts toward greater satisfaction. With the abundant material compiled here, the more you practice, the more adept you'll become at navigating life's twists and turns. Let this guide be your companion as you practice, focus, and integrate affirmations into the seamless flow of the life you wish to create.

The Journey of Affirmations

Now, as you reach the culmination of this collection, you have journeyed through an impressive array of affirmations—233 in total. These include 50 general UHP affirmations, 140 tailored to 23 specific life goals, and 43 crafted around the five guiding principles: focus, belief, simplicity, integration, and proclamation. While the sheer volume may seem overwhelming for daily practice, the key is to choose the affirmations that resonate most deeply with you.

If you're unsure where to start, here's a suggestion:

- For each workday, select one affirmation from each of the five guiding principles. This method keeps things simple and targeted.
- On weekends, you could explore affirmations from the 23 life goals, choosing one from each. This approach offers hours of positive reinforcement that touch every dimension of your personality.

By structuring your practice in this way, you'll find it easy to integrate affirmations into your daily life, making the process both manageable and transformative.

Incorporating Affirmations into Your Routine

The true power of affirmations lies in consistent practice. To begin, select three to five affirmations that resonate with your current goals or aspirations. Here are some examples to consider:

- "I easily attract abundance into every area of my life."
- "I am grateful for my endless supply of daily abundance."
- "I am a creator and attract only positive people, experiences, and financial benefits into my life."

Alternatively, feel free to craft your own affirmations that are deeply personal and aligned with your intentions.

To incorporate affirmations into your routine:

1. **Set Aside Time Daily**: Dedicate a few quiet moments in the morning or before bed to focus on your affirmations.
2. **Combine with Deep Breathing**: Close your eyes and breathe deeply—in through your nose for a count of three, hold for three, and exhale through your mouth for three. This technique enhances focus and relaxation.
3. **Speak Out Loud**: When starting, say your affirmations aloud. The physical act of speaking helps engage your mind and often elicits an emotional response, amplifying their effect. Over time, silently reciting affirmations is fine, but vocalizing them initially creates a stronger impact.

At first, making verbal statements to yourself may feel unfamiliar or even strange. However, research into these psychological techniques shows that affirmations, when practiced correctly, yield incredible results. Many who have adopted this practice swear by its transformative power, especially when integrated into a daily routine.

Remember, the key to success lies in consistency. With practice, your affirmations will become second nature, reshaping your thoughts and life in ways you never imagined.

CHAPTER 8

Overcoming Common Challenges

One of the most profound challenges of affirmations lies in believing in what we cannot yet see in the material world. Manifestation often requires us to trust in the unseen, which can feel uncomfortable or unfamiliar. However, by consistently repeating affirmations, we train our minds to embrace new possibilities and beliefs. As we do so, we begin to challenge what we "know" to be true and expand our perspective.

A helpful way to approach this challenge is to reconnect with your inner child—the version of you unburdened by external limitations. Children live with limitless potential, questioning boundaries and believing in possibilities without hesitation. Reflect on whether, as a child, you placed limits upon yourself, or if those limits were inherited from others. Reclaim that sense of boundless curiosity and faith as you work with affirmations.

Another challenge you may encounter involves situations that test your newly formed beliefs. These moments are opportunities to strengthen your affirmations and align more deeply with your intentions. When faced with such situations, you can:

- **A) Recall your affirmations**: Reiterate the affirmations that ground you in your desired reality.
- **B) Focus on affirmations over fear**: Direct your attention to empowering thoughts instead of allowing fear to take hold.
- **C) Ask for guidance**: Request strength and clarity from the universe to navigate through challenges with grace.

Believing in a reality beyond past experiences takes courage, but with persistence, you can overcome doubt and step into the life you envision.

Dealing with Doubt and Resistance

Doubt and resistance are natural parts of growth and transformation. As you work with affirmations to replace old, unhelpful attitudes, it's important to acknowledge and address the resistance that may arise. These moments of conflict between your external beliefs and new affirmations are opportunities for growth, and with practice, they can be managed effectively.

Techniques to Handle Doubt

1. **Acknowledge Your Doubts**: If you feel intense doubt about a particular affirmation, assertively state the following three times:
   - "If that is true, I can do that, too." This phrase helps bridge the gap between your current belief and your desired reality.
2. **Neutralize Resistance**: When resistance feels overwhelming, you can gently dissipate it by repeating this phrase in a calm, indifferent tone:
   - "I doubt these affirmations are working for me, and I resent having to engage in them to make the changes I feel are necessary." The key is to speak without attach-

ing emotion, allowing the resistance to lose its power and fade away.
3. **Return to Affirmations**: Once doubts have been acknowledged and softened, refocus on your affirmations. Repeat them with intention and belief, reinforcing the positive mindset you are cultivating.

Strengthening Belief

Resistance often arises when new affirmations feel too far removed from your current reality. To strengthen belief:

- Start with affirmations that feel realistic and achievable. Gradually build toward more expansive ones as your confidence grows.
- Pair affirmations with visualization, imagining the outcomes you desire in vivid detail.
- Celebrate small victories along the way, reinforcing your faith in the process.

Remember, doubt is not a sign of failure; it is a natural part of transformation. By addressing resistance with patience and persistence, you pave the way for lasting change.

CHAPTER 9

Advanced Techniques and Strategies

This book serves as both a guide and a celebration of success and abundance. It is the culmination of countless hours spent studying, reading, attending lectures and workshops, and deciphering the intricacies of the world. By reprogramming my mindset to embrace an attitude of expectation, I have cultivated a life of incredible abundance. Through this journey, I've learned that a mindset shift is the fastest, most direct path to unlocking abundance consciousness.

What sets this book apart is its practicality and accessibility. While it contains one of the most comprehensive lists of affirmations available, it doesn't demand acceptance of every technique or strategy. Some advanced practices may not resonate with you right now, and that's okay. Simply reading and absorbing the affirmations can yield profound results, gradually transforming your mindset and opening new doors.

Traditional self-help books often struggle to motivate those who need it most—those seeking an emotional boost just to begin the journey. Happily, this book is different. If you've made it this far, whether reading closely or simply skimming, it's clear you are already seeking ways to elevate your life. My hope is that you'll not only find valuable insights here but also enjoy the process of learning and growing.

Visualization and Affirmation Combos

One of the most potent strategies for achieving success is the combination of visualization and affirmations. This powerful practice enables you to align your conscious and subconscious minds, heightening your awareness and energizing your pursuit of dreams. A compelling example of this comes from Jack Canfield, who taught Jim Carrey the transformative power of visualization. Carrey famously wrote himself a check for ten million dollars and, through a combination of visualization, affirmations, and determination, manifested that dream into reality—eventually becoming the first actor in Hollywood to earn twenty million dollars per movie.

The principle behind this practice is rooted in the ability to energize your physical and emotional self with feelings of hope, joy, and expectancy. By focusing on your goals with intentionality, you create a heightened sensitivity to possibilities and opportunities, paving the way for success.

This powerful combination stimulates neurochemical changes in the brain. Engaging specific neurocircuits with purpose allows you to rewire your mindset and even influence your body at a foundational level. At the quantum level, particles exist as clouds of vibrating energy, influenced by the observer's focus and intent. As Deepak Chopra aptly states, "You have little power when synchronization goes on subconsciously, but enormous power when it goes on consciously." By pairing visualization with affirmations, you consciously direct your energy, aligning your thoughts and actions to achieve remarkable outcomes.

The Quantum Effect and Manifestation

At the submicroscopic level, our very existence is intertwined with waves of energy. Quantum mechanics reveals that observers play an active role in shaping the particles that form the tangible reality around them. In this sense, your presence—your energy—ripples through time and space, exerting a force on quantum possibilities and bringing them into form.

Visualization and affirmation combinations tap into this quantum effect, allowing you to reimagine and reconstruct your reality. By consciously synchronizing your intentions with your actions, you harness the power of quantum mechanics to unlock untold potential.

This practice is about more than simply achieving goals; it's about engaging with life on a deeper level. As you combine imagination, affirmations, and joy, you align yourself with the universe's abundant energy, creating a life that is not only successful but also deeply fulfilling.

CHAPTER 10

Affirmations in Different Areas of Life

As we approach the final steps in this journey of affirmations for abundance—encompassing money, wealth, health, and more—it's worth emphasizing the importance of consistency. Incorporating affirmations into your daily life can amplify your positive mindset, making it second nature. If you find it helpful, consider creating a playlist of affirmations to listen to while eating, cleaning, exercising, or even relaxing. There's never a bad time to reinforce abundance consciousness.

Wealth and Abundance Affirmations:

1. I am living in continual abundance. Wealth flows naturally to me.
2. I am the master of my mind, and I have the right to be wealthy.
3. Money is my friend, and our relationship is harmonious.
4. I view wealth positively—it enriches my life and introduces me to good people.
5. With each passing day, I am becoming wealthier.
6. My dreams are immense, and they deserve great wealth to support them.

7. I transcend the adversity of poverty with grace and strength.
8. I respect and cherish my money, handling it with care, wisdom, and gratitude.
9. I release the past and free myself from frustrations over limited means.
10. From this moment on, I am creating a rich and fulfilling life.
11. I have a clear vision for success, and I am taking meaningful steps toward it.
12. I will reap abundant rewards from my investments in people and opportunities.

Whether you're ready to raise your standard for abundance or still feel some resistance, these affirmations are tools for reprogramming your subconscious mind. Over time, they condition your thoughts and beliefs to align with the abundant life you're creating.

Now, we turn to the last category of affirmations, designed for even deeper reprogramming. These affirmations are interactive—meant to be read aloud, spoken boldly, or even shouted when needed to fully internalize their power.

Spiritual Abundance and Gratitude

Before seeking financial or professional success, it's vital to first give thanks for the gift of life itself. Gratitude creates a foundation for abundance, reminding us of the blessings we already have while attracting more of them into our lives.

Just the act of being alive—breathing, walking, feeling the warmth of the sun, or marveling at nature's beauty—is a testament to our inherent richness. Hugs, laughter, moments of freedom, and simple pleasures like enjoying delicious food or meditating in stillness are all forms of abundance that we often overlook.

Spiritual abundance transcends monetary wealth. True abundance lies in appreciating life's everyday blessings—family, friends, vibrant sunsets, flowing rivers, and the miracle of existence itself. Possessions may be transient, but the gratitude for life's wonders is eternal.

Gratitude Affirmations for Spiritual Abundance:

1. I am grateful for the gift of life and all its blessings.
2. I cherish the beauty of nature, the warmth of the sun, and the flow of rivers.
3. Each moment of laughter, connection, and joy is a treasure in my life.
4. I find peace in stillness, meditation, and the present moment.
5. Gratitude is my guide, attracting abundance into every area of my life.
6. True wealth lies in love, health, and the simple pleasures of existence.
7. I honor and appreciate the miracle of being alive, conscious, and present.

Spiritual abundance reminds us to look beyond material wealth and embrace the richness of life itself. By combining gratitude with intentional affirmations, you align yourself with the universe's generosity, inviting boundless joy, peace, and prosperity.

CHAPTER 11

Maintaining Long-Term Results

Achieving long-term success requires not just initial effort but also the ability to sustain progress over time. This can be accomplished by building strategies that inspire self-motivation and creating a strong foundation of habits and behaviors. Long-term results are about consistency and integrating changes into your lifestyle in ways that feel achievable and rewarding.

For instance, when pursuing goals like weight loss, it's important to focus on sustainable practices. Diets that focus solely on weight loss can be challenging to maintain, but if you shift your attention to finding recipes and foods you genuinely enjoy, the weight loss becomes a natural side effect. This approach makes the process enjoyable and fosters a positive relationship with food.

Key Strategies for Sustaining Results:

- **Pay Attention to Portion Control**: Mindful eating helps prevent overindulgence and promotes a balanced approach to meals.
- **Set Goals for Behavior Modification**: Success comes from building habits that support your long-term vision.

- **Measure Progress Regularly**: Tracking your progress keeps you motivated and provides valuable insights.
- **Embrace New Ideas**: Push beyond your comfort zone to discover creative solutions and fresh perspectives.

Behavior modification plays a central role in maintaining long-term results. This involves creating a lifestyle aligned with your goals, from following a realistic and healthy diet to integrating activities that promote well-being. Small changes, when applied consistently, can lead to significant improvements over time. Scientists have shown that even minor adjustments can create ripple effects that enhance your quality of life.

To begin, assess where you are now. Speak to your doctor, get any necessary tests done, and determine the best course of action for your health or other goals. Remember, the journey is about gradual and sustainable progress—taking the long view ensures lasting success.

Consistency and Persistence

While setting goals is crucial, it's equally important to take the *right* actions toward achieving them. The challenges of information overload and decision fatigue can derail even the best intentions. To stay on track, consider breaking your larger goals into smaller, actionable "mini-goals." These smaller steps require less effort to plan and execute but still contribute meaningfully to your progress.

By focusing on the moment, you reduce overwhelm and create momentum that carries you forward. Before long, these small, consistent efforts add up to significant milestones.

The Importance of Consistent Action:

Napoleon Hill once said, "Success is the result of good judgement; good judgement is the result of experience; experience is often the result of bad judgement." This quote highlights the importance of consistent action as a learning process. When pursuing new goals, it's natural to lack confidence at first. However, taking action—regardless of mistakes—builds experience and leads to better judgment over time.

Building Confidence Through Action:

- **Learn Through Doing**: The act of taking consistent steps allows you to understand the process and gain clarity.
- **Embrace Failure as Growth**: Mistakes are an essential part of learning and refining your approach.
- **Focus on Mini-Wins**: Celebrate small accomplishments to build confidence and motivation.

Conditioning yourself to think successfully is a learned skill, and so is consistently taking action. Start small, stay persistent, and let the process guide you toward achieving your long-term vision.

Conclusion and Final Thoughts

Abundance is not just a concept; it is a mindset that allows us to transcend fear—fear of lack, fear of missing out, and fear of things getting worse. These fears often distort our perspective and prevent us from seeing the possibilities that surround us. An abundance mindset, on the other hand, reminds us that we are all deeply connected to Universal Energy. When we express gratitude for what we have and share our unique talents with the world, we open the door for even greater blessings to flow into our lives.

This is not about chasing unrealistic fantasies or hoping for a magical solution to life's challenges. It is about embracing the truth and beauty of the present, appreciating the opportunities and achievements we experience each day. When we shift our focus to gratitude and abundance, we invite more of the same into our lives. Simply put, when we allow ourselves to be open to receiving abundance, abundance arrives.

Moving Beyond Scarcity Thinking

The world, unfortunately, is steeped in scarcity thinking. Watch the news, and you're likely to encounter narratives of fear, lack, and division. Stories of limited resources and the constant struggle for survival dominate public discourse, shaping a culture of stress and exhaustion. This scarcity mindset pervades not only global conflicts over land and resources but also the everyday grind of going to jobs that deplete us mentally and emotionally.

For many of us, these patterns began early. We grew up watching our parents worry over bills and make sacrifices to provide for the family. These experiences often left us with the belief that struggle and lack are inevitable. But the truth is, this scarcity programming does not define us—it is a story we can rewrite.

By adopting an abundance mindset, we free ourselves from these limiting beliefs. We realize that life is not about competing for finite resources but about sharing in the infinite possibilities that exist. Abundance teaches us to see beyond fear and lack, to trust in the flow of energy and prosperity, and to recognize that we have the power to create a fulfilling and joyous life.

As you close this book, my hope is that you carry forward the principles of abundance with an open heart and a sense of gratitude. This journey has equipped you with affirmations, insights, and tools to reshape your mindset and unlock the life you desire. By focusing on abundance and aligning with Universal Energy, you will discover that the opportunities, connections, and prosperity you seek are already waiting for you—simply step into their flow.

The world may be full of scarcity and doubt, but you have the ability to rewrite your story. Believe in abundance, express your unique gifts, and give thanks for the blessings that surround you. In doing so, you will not only create a life of joy and prosperity for yourself but also inspire others to do the same.

www.ingramcontent.com/pod-product-compliance
Lightning Source LLC
LaVergne TN
LVHW092101060526
838201LV00047B/1510